Financial

Independencewith4 Life

2020 is your year for your finished Internationalesonlines Business

TABLE

hat formatiert
hat formatiert
hat formatiert
hat formatiert
hat formatiert
hat formatiert

0. Introduction

Thank you for making the decision to read this short introduction to this incredible little book to take the first step into a new life. We are not talking about escaping from everyday life completely. Our goal is to build a new way of life that makes your everyday life something you like to experience. What if you could start from scratch? What would you do first?

Many then reply that they would go on holiday immediately, buy a house, invest in the stock market, or buy an expensive status symbol. But this book isn't about holidays or status symbols, it's about your personal lifestyle, which you can drastically change at any time. Design your everyday life according to your individual needs and be your own boss. What does that sound like?

Of course, an optimal life is always a matter of definition. If success means for you to spend a luxurious holiday in the beautiful Maldives and stay in the best hotels, then no one can change it. It's what you want and you should have the freedom to shape your life the way you really want it. Where have you always wanted to go? Use your dreams as motivation to realize your definition of success.

If you've never thought about your deepest desires and dreams, now is the time to take a moment for it. Think carefully about what it is, what you really want in your life. What does your dream reality look like? Is it your desire to travel? Owning a villa? The most expensive car to drive? Using the latest technology? Or do you just want to follow your heart and donate to different organizations? Some want to achieve financial independence in order to spend more time with their families. No matter why you set it your goal, we help you achieve this.

In this book we will introduce you to an efficient method by which all your wish will come true. Gain more time, a community that stands behind you and benefit from the many high-quality products that 4life manufactures. Gain financial independence and become a leader who turns your dreams into goals and thus into their reality. Does all this sound like a dream to you? Make it your everyday life. In this compact book, we show you how to enjoy independence, freedom and an individual way of life.

4life aims to give you a better quality of life and to keep people generally fit. Here we will introduce you to everything there is to know about this company. With the help of the various programs that this interesting company offers, you can become master of your own time. As a result, you no longer fulfill the dreams of others. 4life helps you to realize your own dreams and desires.

You are certainly wondering now how we are going to do that. How can 4life help you find your way to financial independence? Let's introduce the project in more detail in the next pages and discuss the many possibilities that a self-employment with 4life entails. Use the beneficial marketing network to get closer to your definition of success. We will support you at every step and offer you help if you need it.

You will not only get to know the company 4life. We will also address self-employment itself. If you are self-employed, you can enjoy many advantages. Especially if you've never been your own boss, this way of earning a living can seem particularly glamorous. Unfortunately, this is not always the case. This is precisely why 4life is focused on assisting you on your journey to self-employment and supporting you. Do you already know marketing networks? You will be surprised how different 4life is from others.

You will realize for yourself how many benefits this opportunity brings to you today Seize the opportunity and become part of this great project and learn more about online marketing. Let us now go into more detail about the financial independence with 4life.

Enter **YOUR BUSINESS LINK** plus info

1. 4LIFE - TOGETHER, BUILDING PEOPLE

In this book we cover many different topics, which run liket a red thread and connect everything with the company 4life. This diverse company offers many helpful ways to change your own life. Not only the products, but also the opportunities for personal development and financial independence are given. Take advantage of this unique opportunity and do not miss out on your ideal way of life.

First of all, however, I would like to introduce you to the company 4life itself and to introduce you to our history, our philosophy, mission and vision and our products. This helps you understand why we do every day, what we do, and where we want to go in the future. You may want to become part of this exciting project today and turn your own dreams into reality.

4life is based in the United States and specializes in the distribution of dietary supplements. More than 150 permanent employees ensure almost every day that 4life products are of the highest quality. The company also holds some patents to produce the life-enhancing dietary supplement, which is intended to improve your everyday life. We will now take a closer look at all this together.

1.1. Our history

Let's start with how this big company started in the first place. Surprisingly, the long story of 4life begins with a love story. It was David and his wife Bianca Lisonbee who started this project more than 20 years ago. Around this time, you started researching in this sector and created the Transferfactor project. After starting small, their project grew sourandly and research activities increased.

After working with a well-known network marketing company for 11 years, they knew that their project should also go in this direction. The couple knew that this marketing method was the best and most effective they could use for their products. In this way, they introduced various programmes that still benefit people from all over the world. They could be one of them.

After careful study and research, 4life research first opened its doors in 1998. Transferfactor thus became the springboard for all further 4life products and their developments. They went public with the aim of reaching out to as many people as possible and helping their lives to the better. These are all milestones that are far from the past. This many years of experience makes it possible for 4life to reach as many people as possible today. This knowledge is also used to guarantee the highest quality of the products and to be able to offer you the best service.

1.2.   Our vision, mission and long-term goals

In life, it is important to determine a direction. The same applies to a company. It should have a vision, a mission, and long-term goals that point the way and steer towards a better future.

Here at 4life, we attach great importance to creating a better way of life for ourselves and all the people around us and working hard to develop ourselves. Our goal is to increase the physical well-being of our customers and thus make everyday life more pleasant in general. The focus of all our activities is on improving the quality of life. All actions of 4life should serve the good and have a positive influence on this world. People want to live healthier lives, as many trends show. We help you to achieve your best possible quality of life. Our products are there to give you more energy in everyday life and thus to be able to enjoy it better every day.

hat formatiert

Our philosophy ist "Together, Building People". This is English and literally means "together, building people". This alludes to many topics and can be interpreted in different ways. In life, you build relationships that can change everything at lightning speed and open doors that you didn't even notice before. Dietary supplements are also a way to build health and well-being. We have been true to this slogan for decades and will always have a better future as the destination of all our activities. We achieve all of this by working with a wide variety of people to create a community that supports and promotes each other. We want your dreams to come true.

1.3.   Do you already know our products?

As you already know, we attach great importance to providing you with the best possible service and the highest quality when it comes to our products. But what exactly does 4life sell and how are our products manufactured? Let us go into this in more detail.

First of all, let's see what the problem might be. Do you often feel limp or do you often run out of energy at the end of the day? Do you often get sick and don't know why? All of this may be related to your immune system. Our immune system is a complex network that runs through the whole body and effectively protects us from the dangers of everyday life. It works around the clock to keep you well and stay healthy. On the other hand, however, you also have to take proper care of the body, so that this system works properly.

For more than 20 years, we have been producing products that are designed for this purpose. We want to promote a healthy and vital lifestyle so that you get exactly what you deserve. Our decades of experience and the many awards testify to the fact that it really works. Our dietary supplements support your overall well-being and thus improve your quality of life. We also have excellent production facilities and patented processes that guarantee an exclusive food supplement of the highest quality. Take full advantage of life with 4life.

Most of our ingredients, surprisingly, come from cow's milk and chicken eggs. 4life cooperates with many different family farms and farms and accepts only certified dairy products of the highest quality. These follow strict guidelines and quality criteria, which must be observed during production and keeping and must be adhered to. In addition, all our production facilities and farms are regularly inspected by a 4life member. All this in order to offer you the best possible product with the highest quality. Try the products today and see for yourself.

2. THE FIELD OF ACTIVITY OF 4LIFE

Now you know our past, our present and our future. We presented to you how 4life was created, what products we sell and what our vision and mission is. Hopefully, all of this will help you better understand the areas in which 4life is active. Now let's move on to a chapter that describes all the fields of activity we offer alongside our dietary supplements. You will be surprised how diverse our activities are here at 4life. Of course, the focus of the next pages is on what a collaboration with 4life could bring you.

2.1. Our focus is on values

As we briefly mentioned in the previous chapter, a very important aspect of the 4life community is values. Working with colleagues or customers is essential and determines success or failure. We support ourselves and work together towards our goals in order to achieve them faster and easier. Community and camaraderie are the most important values that are of great importance and are promoted by us.

Oursslogan "Together, Building People" is not about s onst. As a consultant at 4life, you become part of a large family that is always there for you and helps you create your dream life. We have made it our goal to serve others. This mentality helps not only you, but also all living beings who cross your path. Rethink and focus on values instead of status symbols. You will see for yourself that this small change of direction in the way of thinking can change your life a lot. Become part of this family and enjoy all the benefits of a community.

2.2. The marketing network with 4life

Our everyday life consists mainly of helping you and supporting you. This is what we do by making products that improve your health. On the other hand, we are a marketing network from which you can clearly benefit. Our unsurpassed rewards plan is unique. We are different from other marketing networks that you may have heard of. While many offer a high reward for New Zu Steiger, at 4life everyone gets a just, high pay.

This means large payouts for all, not just a minority. This sets us apart from most other companies because there is a payout at all levels. This can even be as high as 64 percent, making it the highest sum in the industry. But that is not all. 4life focuses on people and tries to offer the most benefits. Therefore, the payout system has no expiry date. Enjoy endless payouts and become a part of this wonderful community today. We are making sure that everyone gets a fair chance.

2.3. How can you work with us?

You may be wondering how you too can participate in all these wonderful things. Enjoy financial independence by starting your own business with 4life. This method can also be used part-time or as a way of earning 55 to 1000 euros per month. Likewise, it can also be your goal to be able to enjoy the products of 4life practically free of charge. Change your life today and become a professional skilled worker behind you, with a company that will always accompany you on your journey.

They bring motivation and ambition and we do the rest. Enjoy an infinite income with 4life and make your dream of financial independence come true. Take advantage of an existing system that you only have to get into and benefit from decades of experience.

If you are now interested in registering as a specialist consultant, go to the top of the website and enter completely with account details to receive money and add their country hinto . If they are registered now they have a sales link which they can use touse their web sitevto market , in addition ....just click on the link below on thewebsite(application forms on European Consultants) whichopens a form foryou. You can fill it out and sign it to

da-papa-4-you-gmbh@gmx.ch

to forward it to a 4life consultant and also to register internationally. If you have any questions or need more information, you can simply send them to the e-mail da-papa-4-you-gmbh@gmx.ch to the address mentioned. Don't let this chancego en t. Remember that this website belongs to them in three generations and their sales. And it is hereditifier.

2.4. Making real money

What does all this sound like to you?

However, the most crucial question, which is probably very important and interesting for you, has not yet been asked. How can I actually make money with 4life? Can I trust 4life?

We offer 25% on the first order of the frontliner and a uni-level planthat reaches up to 10 generations deep. You can also benefit from the Infinity Bonus , an infiniten additionaln payment. You can also use 2 types of pool participation. Once 1 and once 2% of the company are offered. Since this system has been around for so long, there are also many examples of success. These testify that 4life has the trust of many people who have gone into financial attachment and still enjoy their dream life.

We will, of course, give you a few examples. The top income is earned by Jeff and Michelle Altgilbers, who are paid around 200,000 dollars a month. In second place is Edgar Mojca, who credits 150,000 dollars in commission income per month. Bonnie Taylor came in third place with 95,000 dollars. All this is also possible for you, I will show you how. This method fis not only effective in theory, but also in practice. This is proven by people like Michelle Altgilbers or Edgar Mojca.

2.5. The Power Pool Program

Now you know that you can make real money with 4life. We also offer other things Ergänzthat you should usefor your experience. Our Power Pool program is one of them. Participate in the success of 4life by participating in this program. You can do this once you have become. You have the option to qualify for the Power Pool Program and earn a bonus check for your own personal income. This is a profit share of the monthly profit of the company you earned.

If you are successful in the program for a little longer, you become a teacher who teaches others. This brings you closer to others and helps you improve your leadership and social skills.

In addition, 4life makes regular sweepstakes, in which some consultants and random winners can win a fully paid leave for 2 people in a country of choice.

2.6.   Self-employment as the start of a new life

Have you ever thought about what your dreams and desires are? If so, how do you intend to achieve them? What is important to you in life and where do you want to go? Take a moment to reflect on these important questions. Make a list where you write down everything you want to be or want to do.

If you now think that you will never achieve all this, can I offer you a change of perspective? Instead of looking at the list and despairing, ask yourself how you could do all this. If you had more time? More money? These reasons should not be an obstacle that separates you from your dream life. We not only help you to build your own business, but we also want to learn all the skills you need.

For example, the topic of marketing is something that is becoming more and more important. With this knowledge, we will discuss how you can efficiently market to learn this ability to market yourself and your businesses.

3. FINANCIAL UNABGHÄNGIGKEIT WITH 4LIFE

You may now think that all this is all well and good. But why would I want to be a part of it?

Probably the biggest advantage you will enjoy is financial independence. Benefit from the profits of a company that has been successfully on the market for over 20 years and also has an incredible bonus scheme. This will fulfill your dream of making more money and having less worries.

3.1. Make your dream a reality

What are you dreaming of? Have you ever thought about what your heart wants? Maybe it's more time with the family, romantic outings or holidays for two? Could you also dream of making your everyday life the way you really want it to be? Who does not want to have a positive influence on the world or improve the lives of others?

Treat yourself to all the things you've always had, wanted to do or own. Make your desires and dreams a reality. Become a consultant at 4life and enjoy the many advantages of self-employment. Also experience financial independence with 4life. Once you have reached this level, the doors are open to you. You can drive the most beautiful, most expensive sports car or collect designer handbags. If you wish, you can donate large sums to various organizations or experience excursions and holidays that you did not think possible.

Of course, we are not just striving for material things here. We attach great importance to making sure that you are the best version you can be right now. Personal development is one of our top priorities and, of course, we always support it. Our community is here to help you achieve your dream and make it a reality.

Stop working for the dreams of others and start creating a plan for your own. Realize your deepest heartfelt desires and live the life you have always wanted. There are virtually unlimited possibilities.

3.2. What are the benefits of a company with 4life?

We make your dream areality. Self-employment doesn't just help you make money. Of course, our focus is always on personal development and on providing the best conditions for this. You build something that demands a different side of your personality almost every day. This helps you to develop your skills in a scru't- way. You yourself are your best and most important investment. Never forget that personal growth is the foundation for positive changes in your life.

Basically, you are working on a project that belongs to you alone. Our community is of course always there for you when you need help. Even though you're the boss, you're still building the business with other people, taking advantage of different perspectives and perspectives. This will make the next steps a little easier. You can't create anything great without others. At the end of the day, teamwork always takes you further than you could go alone. If you are a 4life consultant, you too have a positive influence on the lives of your fellow human beings. This is how you help the planet and its inhabitants to have a better future.

In addition to financial independence, you can also fully enjoy the many freedoms that a company brings.

3.3.   Be an entrepreneur

If you now decide to go down this path together with us, I can present to you the many advantages that can be enjoyed if you are an entrepreneur. What is clear is that not everything will always be sugar-coating. They will, of course, also encounter obstacles and perhaps not make any progress. This is precisely why we at 4life are trained to help you and support you on your journey to financial independence. What does the idea of being an entrepreneur sound like to you?

Probably the most important aspect of self-employment is the freedom that can be enjoyed every day. Since the project (WEBSITE) belongs to you alone, you can decide for yourself when, where and how they will work on it. Divide your time according to your ideas and individual needs. On some days, however, this way of life also requires a lot of time and (. That's why we're always there for you. No one deserves high stress or fear of existence.

If you are an entrepreneur, you have your life back in your own hands. You determine where the direction is going and what your everyday life looks like. In addition to the financial and personal freedom that can be enjoyed, there are also some other positive aspects that speak in favour of this project. For example, you have much more opportunities to develop yourself and learn a variety of skills.

3.4.   Online Marketing

As mentioned several times, we want to promote your personal development as much as possible and help you become the best version of your own person. An important aspect of this task is to promote and always improve your own skills. This is crucial to be satisfied and happy in the world of work, as well as in private life. Growing constantly improves your quality of life enormously.

If you then concentrate on gaining skills that will definitely be in demand in the future, you will set yourself a path. A path to a better way of life that offers many different opportunities and opportunities. After all, if you know how to make money now and continue to develop your skills, almost nothing can go wrong financially. You have done everything in your power.

Online marketing is a skill that is in high demand today. In the future too, we believe that this area of marketing is becoming increasingly important. However, this topic is not only important in order to bring your products to the man and introduce it to as many people as possible. Marketing is also important to market yourself or pitch an idea. Learn how to communicate your thoughts so that your counterpart is interested or may even participate in your project.

Learn everything you needto know to become self-employed and learn the marketing principles with our support. Forthefuture, learn more about the important topic Online Marketing , And 4Life.

Here your Info Link

The successful product of the Team Cash Flow Marketing:

Cash Flow Ads 2.0

How Facebook Marketing works in 2019 and what 95% of all marketers do wrong. How you can securely unlock profitable Facebook Ads Pay-Per-Click advertising and build a business like that.

3.5. How to make your dream come true

Now you know the main ways you can work with 4life. Do you think this project is helpful? Do you perhaps see potential for the future in the company 4life? We want to help you develop your dream life. You should be able to enjoy every day of your life and follow the enthusiasm and the urge for new things.

As a 4life consultant, we make your dreams come true. The principle is very simple. Ultimately, it's just a matter of getting the motivation and the will to work on something big every day. Understand that we are working together on a huge project that basically pays everyone. This system is fair and fair. Benefit from the success of a company that has been operating at a profit for decades and specializes in helping others and shaping a better future.

We would like to have you on board 4life. This way you can not only use the products themselves. You will also benefit from all the listed benefits and end up with something that no one can take away from you. Especially your personal skills and experience are something you can use throughout your life.

If you are now interested in becoming part of this project yourself, you can contact us here

Register here as a customer advisor. After the purchase, they will receive an e-mail and they can register as customer advisors and Wmarket their finished product page themselves withtheir tailored marketing link.

You will find a link on the website at the bottom left that will direct you to a document. You can easily fill in this application and send it to da-papa-4-you-gmbh@gmx.ch. One of our competent skilled workers will then take care of your registration.

In addition, you get from us a marketing tool with everything you need for online marketer product marketing and more for professionals or beginners, they immediately put on

business, here their link to the online marketing tool.

And here is a free Info product Turbo Tool **BOX**

4. WHAT ARE THE ADVANTAGES OF THIS SYSTEM?

Now that we've looked at 4life and its fields of activity and explained how this marketing network works, it's time to take a closer look at the many benefits you have with 4life. We will focus on 3 main aspects and discuss how this point will change your life and change for the better. First of all, we will talk about the freedom that self-reliance brings. Then we get to the point that this system gives us the chance to do more, and finally we will cover how precisely we can now shape a better future for all. We hope that everything about our

---

hat formatiert

Feldfunktion geändert

hat formatiert

hat formatiert

hat formatiert

hat formatiert

hat formatiert

hat formatiert

hat formatiert

hat formatiert

Feldfunktion geändert

hat formatiert

hat formatiert

hat formatiert

hat formatiert: Schriftart: (Standard) +Textkörper (Calibri),

hat formatiert: Schriftart: (Standard) +Textkörper (Calibri),

Feldfunktion geändert

hat formatiert: Schriftart: (Standard) +Textkörper (Calibri),

hat formatiert

hat formatiert

project will be clear to you and that we have been able to convince you to think about becoming self-employed with 4life.

4.1.Freedom

Probably the biggest advantage of a company of your own is the many freedoms it entails. Because as an entrepreneur, you are independent. You are free, stand on your own two legs and can be proud of your successes, as only you are responsible for them. Of course, this also means that you are also responsible for the failure of a project. Freedom is not just an advantage. You have to learn self-discipline and motivation to make the effort that is in front of you every day. If you don't want to do this or work into the day without a goal, you may not get very far in general.

Enjoy complete independence. This allows you to design and be able to design your everyday life completely freely and to decide for yourself when and how you want to work. They are no longer tied to fixed working hours. Create a plan or process that is perfectly tailored to your personal needs. So you can effectively divide your time and do what you really want to do, ifyou want to.

You can also decide in which environment you want to work. For some, it's easiest when they work at their kitchen table and to this one every day. Maybe you're more of the type who is looking for variety and also likes to work in the park if you just want to. No matter how you structure your everyday life, don't let anyone dictate anything and enjoy your life as you prefer.

Never let other people decide what your everyday life looks like. Choose your place of work and time. As long as you do the work, it doesn't matter how you do it, you should feel comfortable with it and choose an environment that helps you focus and work effectively. Do you already know this place? If not, consider where you can best focus and try to use this place for your work.

The many freedoms is definitely a very big advantage of self-employment. If you sign up as a consultant at 4life today, you have the chance to fully enjoy this aspect. What does that sound like to you?

4.2.Opportunity for more

In addition to the many freedoms and the possibility of being able to divide one's time completely, there is a chance for more. What do we mean by that? Let us take a closer look at this advantage and see how you too can take advantage of the opportunity to do more.

What would you do if you could enjoy financial independence tomorrow? Most people often reply that you would like to go on holiday or generally want to travel a lot. This is all well and good and should be fully exploited. But this idea is very short-term. An average holiday lasts one to two weeks. And then? What will you do with your life after your first desire to travel?

Think a little longer term. What will your life look like after the first gland of financial independence has subsided? What are you going to do then?

As a 4life consultant, you have the chance to do more. This basically means that you are not limited from a financial point of view. Self-employment is the only way in which you can earn as much as you want in theory. This opens some doors and gives you opportunities that you probably haven't even heard of yet. Travel and holidays are a way to fulfill your dreams.

hat formatiert

You may not want to travel at all, but rather invest in a new car. Treat yourself to all the material things you've always wanted. When you have reached a certain level of self-employment, there is almost nothing you could not buy. What have you always dreamed of? A house in Italy? A personal sailboat? A designer handbag?

But don't get too caught up in these thoughts. After all, material things are beautiful toys that will eventually lose interest. Think about what you would do if you died tomorrow. Would your car be the most important to you? Probably not. Your family, friends and health will then be your focus. But that should be the case now.

Enjoy all the material things you want, but never forget your most important values.

4.3.A better future for all

There is a vision behind every successful company. A dream that someone has pursued and realized. Do you have bigger visions of what the future looks like?

A better future is a noble life goal that not many have. Nevertheless, it is very important, otherwise almost nothing would be possible. Most companies are driven to change the morning. They want to publish groundbreaking technologies, submit patents for processes that are in demand in the future or help people in need. If this mindset did not exist, everything would go down the creek pretty quickly. Our society and our economy would not function in this way. A company usually sets this philosophy in its vision. It is a slogan, a thought or a guide that is intended to lead in a certain direction.

Your daily decisions should also be made in order to create a better future for you and your fellow human beings. So you move forward and do something good for yourself and the world. This guarantees constant personal growth, which regularly includes a new version of your person.

hat formatiert

At 4life, we attach great importance to this aspect and help you to really live this philosophy. For example, our products are designed to improve your well-being and health. Of course, this does not happen within a day. You should use the supplements regularly to enjoy all the benefits and positive effects. That's why we always think about tomorrow when making our products. Can our means help you to be healthy and fit tomorrow? It is important to us to have a clear vision for the future. That's why we put so much effort into our consultants.

It is important to us that we can build a better life and a brighter future together with you. Live the life you've always wanted and earned. If you keep your dreams and goals in mind every day, they will burn into your memory and subconsciously you will always approach them.

Become part of this exciting project today that will allow you to benefit greatly. Together we create a better future for all.

Here is an e-mail marketing tool for Info

Feldfunktion geändert

hat formatiert: Schriftart: (Standard) +Textkörper (Calibri),

hat formatiert: Schriftart: (Standard) +Textkörper (Calibri),

hat formatiert: Schriftart: (Standard) +Textkörper (Calibri),

THE MOST IMPORTANT THINGS AT A GLANCE

Finally, we would like to round off this book by presenting the most important details, information and facts clearly. What did you find particularly interesting? Would you like to learn more about 4life? What does all this sound like to you?

All in all, it can be said that every year thousands of people are enthusiastic about working with 4life. On the Internet you will find many reviews and testimonials that underline this. There are already a lot of people who have made your dream a reality and are now enjoying their dream life right now. You can also easily be a part of this wonderful community and make a life-changing decision. See for yourself and find out how far you can go. What are your limits?

What inspires you? Why would you like to be self-employed? What dreams and desires are there to realize in your life? Think about where you want to go in your life. Make a list of all the things you want to achieve in this life. You can then use these as motivation and always resort to them when the project comes to a halt or demands a lot from you. Take a step forward and move on to your dream life.

Benefit from 4life's decades of experience. We have been at the forefront of dietary supplement research and production for over 20 years. You can do this to your advantage by taking advantage of the opportunities available. The path is designed for you, you just have to take the first step and get started. Not only the many experiences, but also the growing community are something that you can use for your projects.

In addition, you get from us a marketing tool with everything you need for online marketer productvermartung and more for professionals or beginners, they set the same

on Finished International Online Business website your link and with additional information ,LINK

More information about the 4LIFE company

LINK1 4life company presentation

LINK3, LINK4 , Link5 , LINK6

Great products for incredible success

hat formatiert: Englisch (Vereinigte Staaten)

how would you make your life more rewarding?

Would you get rid of all your debts? Would you spend more time with your loved ones instead of working for an ordinary salary? Would you try to help others make their lives worthwhile? Would you like to start today ? You can do that - with the marketing plan.

VIDEO 4LIFE Video 2 Video 3 Video 4

The 4life community supports you every step of the way and gives you as much advice as possible to help you move forward. We dream of a near future in which everyone can live according to their own ideas and enjoy financial independence. You too deserve your deepest wishes and dreams to come true. You know exactly what you want and how you can achieve it. Why don't you start today? What keeps you from pursuing your dreams?

We would like to have you on board 4life. This way you can not only use the products themselves. You will also benefit from all the listed benefits and end up with something that no one can take away from you. Especially your personal skills and experience are something you can use throughout your life.

If you are now interested in becoming part of this project yourself, you cansign up here .

Here entrepreneurs are MADE TO BE ,

to enter your website . In addition, you will find a link on the website at the bottom, unten finden,

the (application forms to European Consultants) which directs them to the document and must be completed. You can easily fill in this application and send it to da-papa-4-you-gmbh@gmx.chfor additionalinternationalregistration. One of our competent skilled workers will then take care to complete your registration.

In addition, you get from us a marketing tool with alln what you need for online marketer product marketing and more for professionals or beginners, put them right on business,

here their link

We look forwardarto welcoming them to **our community as expert advisors.** .

INFO PRODUCTS
with LINK.

COACHY - Your member area with Landingpage Builder!

It's never been so easy!

With Coachy, you can create your own member area for your digital products. The creation and operation is extremely easy and therefore 10x faster than with WordPress and other solutions!

- ▶ **More than 3,000 coaches are already** working with it!
- ▶ On Facebook we only have 5-star reviews!
- ▶ influencers and well-known personalities like **Calvin Hollywood, Simon Mathis** and **Oliver Sievers** use Coachy!

Strandbusiness 2.0 One-time payment

Turnkey affiliate project
50% Commission=74€ per sale!

23

with one-off payment otherwise distributed on 4 instalments NEW!!
YOUR OWN BEACH BUSINESS

Description for customers:
You will get a complete pre-installed turnkey affiliate blog including 10 ready-made review pages of high-turnover affiliate products. Earn a whopping commission per sale every month, all fully automatic.

The 5000 Euro Tip

I will show you how I set up a system in just 3 hours with which I earn
5000 Euros per month and how you can implement it immediately!

Affiliate Toolkit (Premium Wordpress Plugin)

The plugin makes it easy to create and maintain products and lists. You work with your own templates and custom fields. In addition, there is also a WooCommerce interface.

This plugin allows you to quickly insert affiliatelinks and entire lists. The buyer can immediately start building his website.

We use the plugin ourselves and constantly develop it for interesting functions.

The current list of functions can always be found here:

Imprint

Owner Marcus Ronneberger / Lucidie - Company da papa 4 you gmbh

www.ingramcontent.com/pod-product-compliance
Lightning Source LLC
LaVergne TN
LVHW091202050326
832903LV00041B/519